Bridges Out of Poverty

Strategies for Professionals and Communities

Workbook

Philip DeVol, Ruby K. Payne, and Terie Dreussi Smith
   Bridges Out of Poverty: Strategies for Professionals and Communities Workbook
      100 pp.
   Bibliography 69–70
   ISBN 13: 978-1-934583-59-3
   ISBN 10: 1-934583-59-6
   Excerpted from *Bridges Out of Poverty: Strategies for Professionals and
      Communities; Getting Ahead in a Just-Gettin'-By World: Building Your
      Resources for a Better Life; A Framework for Understanding Poverty*

   1. Education   2. Sociology   3. Title

Copy editing by Dan Shenk
Book design by Paula Nicolella
Cover design by ArtLink, Inc.

Other titles from aha! Process, Inc.

   Bridges Out of Poverty: Strategies for Professionals and Communities by Philip
      DeVol, Ruby K. Payne, and Terie Dreussi Smith

   Bridges Out of Poverty: Strategies for Professionals and Communities Video Series

   A Framework for Understanding Poverty by Ruby K. Payne

   Getting Ahead in a Just-Gettin'-By World by Philip DeVol

   Facilitator Notes for Getting Ahead in a Just-Gettin'-By World by Philip DeVol

   Investigations Into Economic Class in America by Philip DeVol and Karla M. Krodel

   Jodi's Stories by Jodi Pfarr

BRIDGES OUT OF POVERTY

Strategies for Professionals and Communities

Workbook

Philip DeVol
Ruby K. Payne
Terie Dreussi Smith

Contents

Introduction   vii

Mental Models   1

Research Continuum   17

Key Points   25

Hidden Rules   27

Language   33

Resources   45

Bibliography—Suggested Reading   69

Additive Model   71

Introduction

Much has changed since *Bridges Out of Poverty* was first published in 1999.

At that time the U.S. Welfare Reform Act of 1996 appeared to be producing impressive results. TANF (Temporary Assistance to Needy Families) caseloads had been cut in half, poverty and unemployment rates were at record lows, and there were substantial increases in the income levels of single-mother families. When the technology-driven economic boom ended in early 2000 it became apparent to poverty watchers, if not the media or the general public, that the gains were more a function of a strong economy than the welfare reform policy. When the attention of the nation shifted to terrorism and wars, people in poverty became invisible again, almost as invisible as they were in the 1950s.

Now, with a dubious debt of gratitude to Hurricane Katrina in 2005, poverty in the United States became visible again. Katrina blew away the generally held belief that welfare reform was a success and the U.S. economy was working for everyone. Even the popular media began raising questions about race and class.

But Katrina did more than make poverty visible again; it also has served as a metaphor for poverty itself. The storm threw communities into chaos, forcing community organizations, as well as individuals, into survival mode. Basic community resources such as housing, health care, education, police, transportation, and utilities were wiped out or severely disrupted. Community structures and budgets were overwhelmed. Similar language can be used to describe the impact of poverty on families. Poverty itself throws families into chaos, forcing them into survival mode. Basic resources are wiped out or severely disrupted. Family structures and budgets are inadequate and overwhelmed. Furthermore, the Katrina metaphor can be used to describe some cities and rural communities. The difference between a natural disaster and the poverty disaster is this: For people and communities in poverty, the crisis tends to creep along in obscurity rather than front and center, day after day, in the news.

So what were the results of welfare reform, and what has happened since 2000 when the economic boom ended? Even though the minimum wage was raised four times during the 1990s, the arithmetic of life was still not working for people at the bottom of the ladder. In 1999 about 42% of persons considered poor *worked* and were still living in poverty. Poverty rates are up. From 2000 to 2005 the number of people in poverty in the United States rose 17%. In 2004 an additional 1.1 million people fell into poverty; it was the fourth year in a row that poverty numbers had grown. In 2004 there were 37 million people in poverty. The U.S Bureau of Labor Statistics reported in December 2004 that 25% of all the jobs in the U.S. economy did not pay enough to lift a family above the poverty line. In some states 30% of all jobs did not pay a living wage. This country has become a nation where people can work full time and still be in poverty. Amy Glasmeier, in *An Atlas of Poverty in America*, sums up the current situation: "… [T]he experiment of the 1990s … has resulted in a growth in income poverty [as opposed to net-worth poverty] that leaves the nation's must vulnerable members unprotected from economic uncertainty and insecurity."

The Katrina metaphor can be used to illustrate how people respond to disasters and to poverty. To survive Katrina, people used reactive and sensory skills to solve immediate and concrete problems. There's nothing abstract about keeping your head above water or finding food or shelter. Solving problems minute-by-minute, day-by-day with limited resources is a valuable survival skill that people in poverty possess. In a crisis of a relatively short duration—such as hurricanes, tsunamis, and earthquakes—concrete, reactive problem solving is eventually replaced by abstract, proactive strategies that are based on future ramifications. This is the experience of many middle-class and wealthy people caught in the upheaval and chaos of natural disasters. For folks in poverty, on the other hand, natural disasters create a double whammy. First, there is the disaster itself, after which the unrelenting and unending crisis, as experienced in poverty, forces people into the tyranny of the moment. This is where the future is lost, where people get stuck solving the same problems over and over, and where proactive planning is difficult to do.

Individuals in poverty aren't alone in this trap; many communities across the U.S. are so busy responding to crises that they too are using reactive strategies to survive. The same can be said of nations where poverty rates are extremely high.

People at the very bottom of the economic ladder aren't the only ones in trouble. For the first time in U.S. history, the middle class is shrinking. The median household income has been flat for five straight years, and only the top 5% of households experienced real income gains in 2004. The structures that created the middle class—well-paying jobs, the 40-hour workweek, assistance with college loans and home mortgages, and employer-provided health care and pensions—are falling away.

The economic insecurity of low-wage workers and the middle class threatens the viability of our communities. When members of the middle class flee the cities, taking the tax base and spending power with them … when Main Street empties of viable businesses and refills with pawn shops, used clothing stories, social service storefronts, and payday lenders … when people can't afford to stay in the community to raise their children because of the lack of well-paying jobs … and when the free and reduced-price lunch rate at the schools hits 50%, our communities are becoming unsustainable.

Our work is to improve the lives of people in poverty and, by extension, to help make sustainable communities in which everyone can do well. In this edition of *Bridges Out of Poverty* you will find an essay titled "The Additive Model: The aha! Process Approach to Developing Sustainable Communities." It expands on the ideas introduced here and lays out the philosophy behind our work. In it you will read about:

- Using the knowledge of people in poverty to build an accurate mental model of poverty.
- Studying poverty research in order to develop a continuum of strategies for building prosperous and healthy communities.
- Theories of change.
- The additive model and how it applies to aha! Process constructs.
- Sharing aha! Process constructs with people in poverty.
- Creating sustainable communities.

Bridges Out of Poverty is a starting point where one can develop accurate mental models of poverty, middle class, and wealth. It is a new lens through which readers can view themselves, their clients, and the community. Readers can begin to work on front-line staff skills and to develop new program designs in order to improve relationships and outcomes. The purpose is to give community leaders from all disciplines a start on that path. Hundreds of thousands of professionals in education, social services, healthcare, law enforcement, corrections, business, and government already have been exposed to and inspired by Dr. Ruby K. Payne's understanding of economic diversity. Many towns, cities, and counties—and some states—have begun making changes that come from her ideas, techniques, and approaches to change.

We hope this book will contribute to the good work you are doing.

Philip DeVol
July 2006

GUIDING PRINCIPLE

The mission of aha! Process, Inc. is to positively impact the education and lives of individuals in poverty around the world.

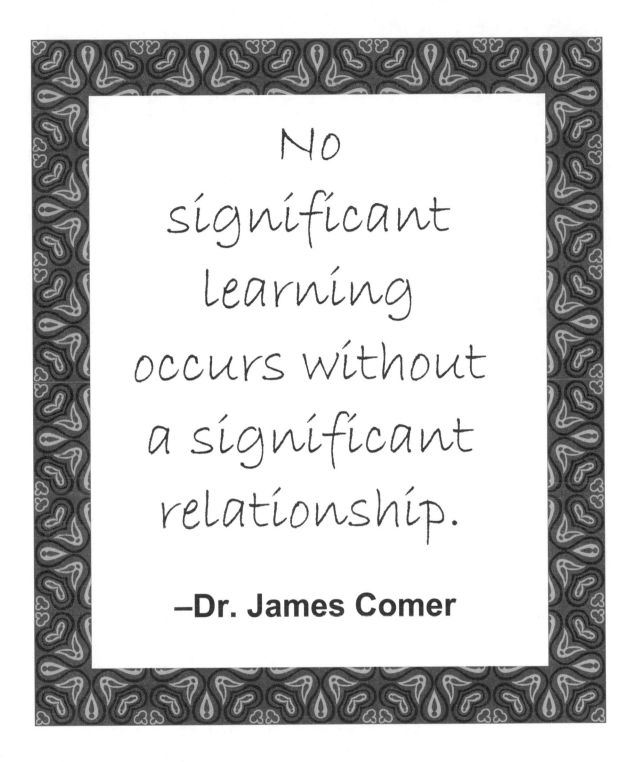

No significant learning occurs without a significant relationship.

–Dr. James Comer

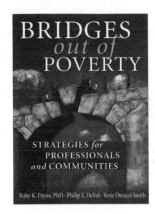

Mental Models

OBJECTIVES

- Explore the concrete experience of people in generational poverty.

- Create a mental model of poverty.

- Analyze elements of the model.

- Create a mental model of middle class.

- Understand the interlocking nature of the models and the demands of the environment.

Mental Models ...

- Are an internal picture of how the world works

- Exist below awareness

- Are theories-in-use, often unexamined

- Determine how we act

- Can help or interfere with learning

For a dialogue to occur we must suspend our mental models.

www.ahaprocess.com

Mental Model for Poverty:
What It's Like Now

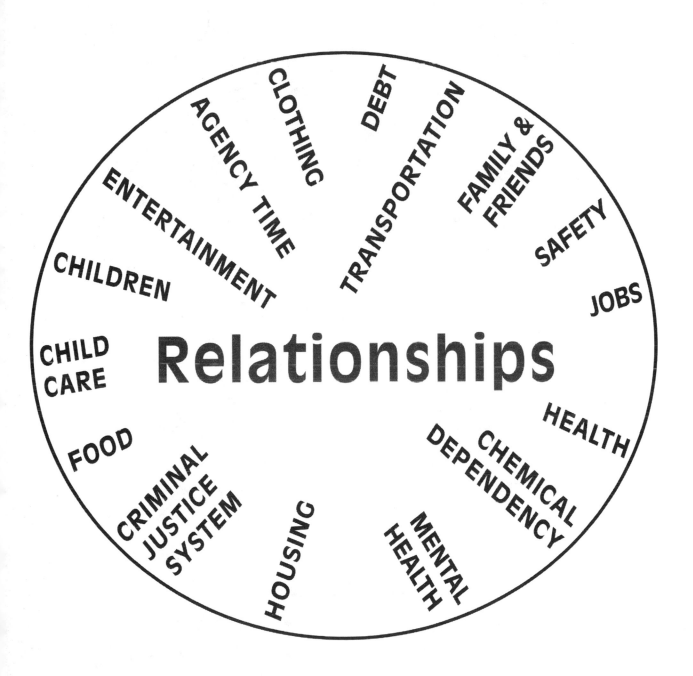

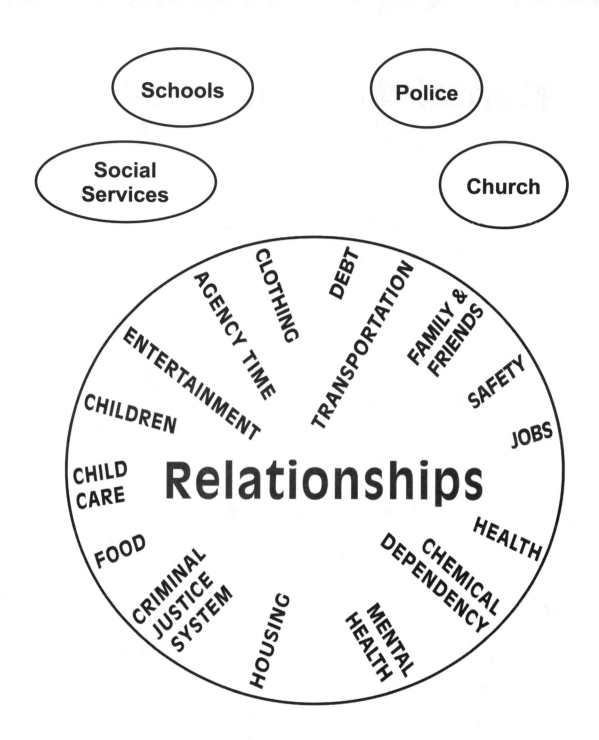

Schools

Police

Social Services

Church

Relationships

AGENCY TIME

CLOTHING

DEBT

TRANSPORTATION

FAMILY & FRIENDS

SAFETY

JOBS

ENTERTAINMENT

CHILDREN

CHILD CARE

FOOD

CRIMINAL JUSTICE SYSTEM

HOUSING

MENTAL HEALTH

CHEMICAL DEPENDENCY

HEALTH

Businesses

- Pawn shop
- Liquor store
- Corner store
- Rent to own
- Laundromat

- Fast food
- Check cashing
- Temp services
- Used-car lots
- Dollar store

Housing Trends

1991

47 affordable rental units per 100 low-income families

1997

36 affordable rental units per 100 low-income families

Source: "Rental Housing—the Worsening Crisis: A Report to Congress on Worst-Case Housing Needs" *(March 2000), U.S. Housing & Urban Development*

Housing Trends

	Number of low-income families	Number of low-income rental units available
1970	7.3 million	9.7 million
1985	11.6 million	7.9 million

Source: Prosperity Lost *(1990) by Philip Mattera*

www.ahaprocess.com

59% of poor renters spend more than 50% of their income on shelter.

Source: "Why America's Workers Can't Pay the Rent" *(Summer 2000) by Peter Dreier in* Dissent

- 22% of U.S. workers earn less than $8 an hour.

- 29 million U.S. workers hold jobs for at least half a year and earn less than $15,000.

- Median net worth for top 10%: $833,600

- Median net worth for bottom 20%: $7,900

Source: David Shipler, Stanford Social Innovations Review *(Summer 2004)*

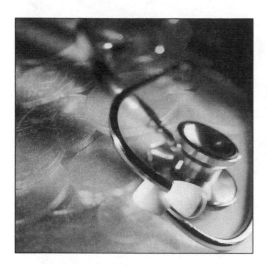

Co-Investigating Health Issues

- **The SES (socioeconomic status) Gradient**
- **The richer you are the healthier you are.**
- **The poorer you are the sicker you are.**
- **Living in poverty is a risk factor for stress-related illnesses.**
- **It is NOT entirely due to lack of access.**

Source: Why Zebras Don't Get Ulcers *(1998) by Robert Sapolsky*

It's Due to Social Coherence

"Does a person have a sense of being linked to the mainstream of society, of being in the dominant subculture, of being in accord with society's values?"

"Can a person perceive society's messages as information, rather than as noise? In this regard, the poor education that typically accompanies poverty biases toward the latter."

"... has a person been able to develop an ideal set of coping responses for dealing with society's challenges?"

"... does a person have the resources to carry out plans?"

"... does a person get meaningful feedback from society—do their messages make a difference?"

–Robert Sapolsky, Aaron Antonovsky

Tyranny of the Moment

"The need to act overwhelms any willingness people have to learn."

Source: The Art of the Long View *by Peter Schwartz*

"The healthier you are psychologically, or the less you may seem to need to change, the more you can change."

Source: Management of the Absurd *(1996) by Richard Farson*

Mental Model for
Middle Class

www.ahaprocess.com

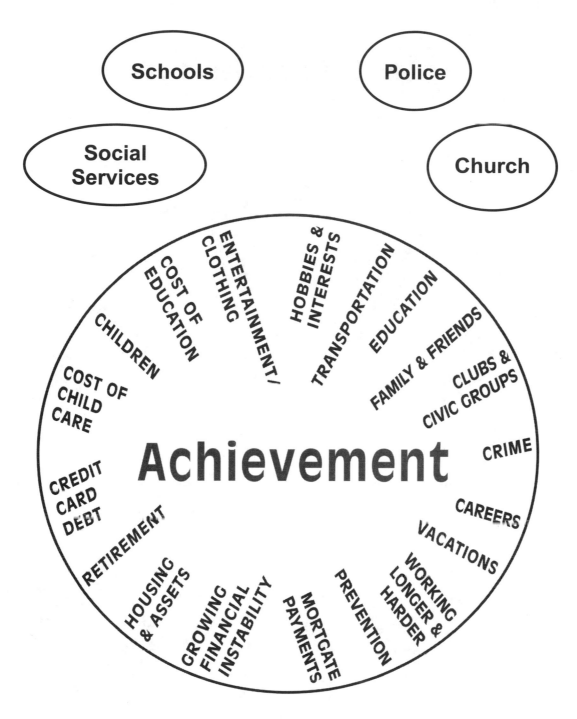

Schools

Police

Social Services

Church

ENTERTAINMENT/ CLOTHING

COST OF EDUCATION

CHILDREN

HOBBIES & INTERESTS

TRANSPORTATION

EDUCATION

FAMILY & FRIENDS

COST OF CHILD CARE

CLUBS & CIVIC GROUPS

Achievement

CRIME

CREDIT CARD DEBT

CAREERS

VACATIONS

RETIREMENT

HOUSING & ASSETS

GROWING FINANCIAL INSTABILITY

MORTGATE PAYMENTS

PREVENTION

WORKING LONGER & HARDER

Businesses

- Shopping/strip malls
- Bookstores
- Banks
- Fitness centers
- Vet clinics

- Office complexes
- Coffee shops
- Restaurants/bars
- Golf courses

Mental Model for
Wealth

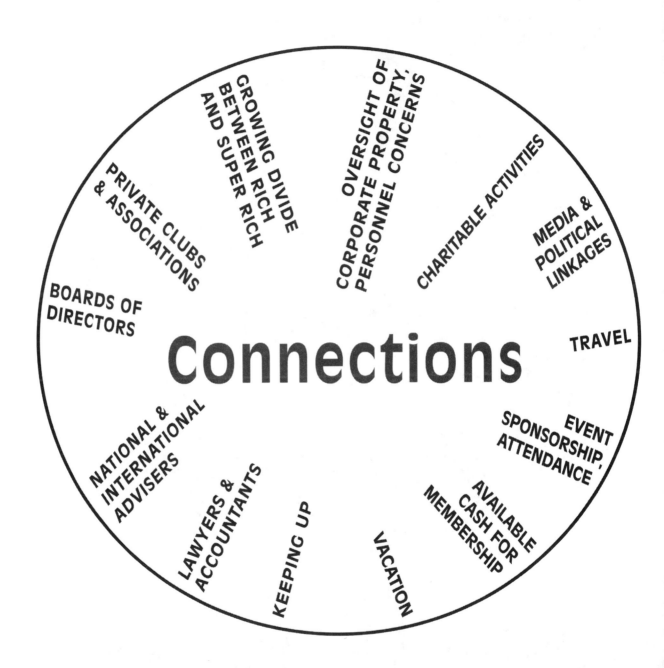

www.ahaprocess.com

Mental Model of Generational Poverty

- It is a description of the concrete experience.

- It is an abstract representation of poverty.

- It depicts vulnerability.

- It depicts the relative importance and interlocking nature of the elements.

- It is a depiction of the trap: no future story, no choice, no power.

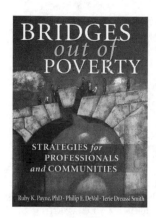

Research
Continuum

OBJECTIVES

- **Understand the many causes of poverty in order to assist people in poverty to build resources.**

- **Understand what is needed to build sustainable communities.**

Poverty Research Continuum

CAUSES	Behaviors of the Individual	Absence of Human and Social Capital	Human Exploitation	Political/ Economic Structures
RESEARCH TOPICS	Dependence on welfare Criminal Behavior Dropping out of school Single parenthood Intergenerational character traits Bad mothers, mother-centered, matriarchal structures Values held by poor, lack of work ethic, commitment to achievement Breakup of families INDIVIDUAL CIRCUMSTANCES Disabilities Addiction, mental illness, domestic violence	Lack of employment Lack of education Inadequate skill sets Decline in neighborhoods Big government Decline in social morality Urbanization Suburbanization of manufacturing "White flight" Inelastic cities: inadequate regional planning Immigration Failure of social services Absence of knowledge, worker skills, intellectual capital Social capital Lack of career ladder between knowledge and service sectors Speed of economic transformation at local level	Minimum wage vs. living wage Temporary jobs Less than 30 hours Lack of benefits Disposable employees Debt bondage Global outsourcing Payday lenders Lease/purchase Redlining Drug trade Exploitation for markets Exploitation of resources and raw materials	Policies that result in economic and social disparity Undue influence of corporations on legislation Tax structure that shifted tax burden to middle class, away from wealthy and corporations Decline in wages for bottom 90% Decline of unions De-industrialization Management/labor "bargain" CEO-to-line-worker salary ratio Profit/financial-centered form of globalization

Poverty Research Continuum
(continued)

CAUSES	Behaviors of the Individual	Absence of Human and Social Capital	Human Exploitation	Political/ Economic Structures
ASSUMPTIONS	By studying the poor, we will learn what changes individuals must make in order to climb out of poverty. The poor are somehow lacking, either by their own bad choices or by circumstances. They should become "like us." Poverty is a sustainable condition.	By studying human and social capital, we will learn how to work within the larger political/ economic structure to create conditions that foster prosperity. Faith that the market and market corrections will create most of the conditions necessary for general prosperity Acceptance of a 4 to 5% unemployment rate as an acceptable feature of the economy	By studying colonial and imperialist behavior, we can learn how to create just and equitable economic structures. Dominant groups discount the legitimacy of this category and look to the future. Dominated people (Appalachian, African Americans, Native Americans, former colonies) remember the past and may seek redress.	Studying the poor is not the same thing as studying poverty. Race, class, and gender are categories for analysis, not just demographics.
WHAT'S SAID	Don't blame the system; change the individual. Don't upset the system.	Don't blame the political/ economic system; change the individual and the community system.	Upset the system and make it fair.	Don't blame the individual. Change the political/ economic structure; fight poverty instead of reforming welfare.

Poverty Research Continuum

(continued)

CAUSES	Behaviors of the Individual	Absence of Human and Social Capital	Human Exploitation	Political/ Economic Structures
SAMPLE FACTS	Number of words heard by age 3 by children in welfare, working class, and professional homes: 10 million, 20 million, and 30 million words, respectively. Prohibitions-to-encouragements ratio in responses to children in welfare, working class, and professional homes: 2:1, 1:2, 1:5, respectively. Average vocabulary of children at age 3 years in professional homes is 1,200 words. For adults in welfare homes it is 900 words used commonly in conversation (Hart/Risley). In 1960, for every 100 African-American single mothers there were 413 married couples; in 1995 for every 100 single mothers there were 63 married couples. Whites: 100 to 1,539 in 1960 and 100 to 422 in 1995 (Rusk).	"… [A]lmost 30 percent of the workforce toils for $8 an hour or less, as the Washington-based Economic Policy Institute reported in 1998 …" (Ehrenreich). National Coalition for the Homeless, 1997: Nearly one-fifth of all homeless people in 29 cities are employed in full- or part-time jobs (Ehrenreich).	Developing countries send developed countries 10 times as much money through unequal trade and financial relations as they receive through foreign aid (United Nations). Eighty-four percent of the world's children are raised in poverty on income of less than $2 a day (Galeano). The United States represents 5% of the world's population—and uses 50% of the world's resources. Racism	"According to the National Coalition for the Homeless, in 1998 … it took, on average nationwide, an hourly wage of $8.89 to afford a one-bedroom apartment; the Preamble Center for Public Policy was estimating that the odds against a typical welfare recipient's landing a job at such a 'living wage' were about 97 to 1" (Ehrenreich). Economic disparity—top 10% getting richer, bottom 90% getting poorer—has been a growing trend since the 1970s (Brouwer). Tax shift from corporations to individuals: The 1940s corporations paid 33%, individuals 44%. The 1990s corporations paid 14%, individuals 73% (Brouwer).

Poverty Research Continuum

(continued)

CAUSES	Behaviors of the Individual	Absence of Human and Social Capital	Human Exploitation	Political/ Economic Structures
SOURCES, RESEARCH INSTITUTES, ANALYSTS, WEBSITES	Michael Harrington, Betty Hart and Todd Risley, Oscar Lewis, Daniel Patrick Moynihan, Charles Murray, Jack Pransky American Enterprise Institute Brookings Institution Bureau of Applied Research, Columbia University Council for Urban Affairs Department of Social Relations, Harvard University Ford Foundation Heritage Foundation Institute for Social Research, University of Michigan Manhattan Institute University of Chicago www.financeproject.org www.heritage.org	David Brooks, Robert Lampman, John McKnight, Daniel Patrick Moynihan, Gunnar Myrdal, Robert Putnam, David Rusk, William Wilson American Council on Education Bureau of Applied Research, Columbia University Department of Social Relations, Harvard University Ford Foundation Institute for Social Research, University of Michigan University of Chicago University of Wisconsin, IRP Urban Institute www.childwelfare.com www.clasp.org www.cpmcnet.columbia. edu/dept/nccp/index.html www.mdrc.org www.urban.org www.welfareinfo.org www.wmadcampaign.org	Saul Alinksy, Kenneth Clark, Eduardo Galeano, Jim Goad, Margaret Hagood, Charles S. Johnson, Harvey Wasserman Economic Policy Institute of National Emergency Council www.northwestern.edu	Steve Brouwer, David Caplovitz, Osha Davidson, Hernando De Soto, Robert Frank, B. Franklin Frazier, Paulo Freire, John Kenneth Galbraith, Herbert Gans, Graham Hancock, Michael Harrington, Bell Hoods, Marjorie Kelly, Christopher Lasch, Charles Lewis, Robert Putnam, Robert Sapolsky, Muhammad Yunus Center for Budget and Policy Priorities Urban Institute www.acorn.org www.bettercommunities. org www.bread.org www.fair.org www.nlihc.org www.ufenet.org

Poverty Research Continuum

(continued)

CAUSES	Behaviors of the Individual	Absence of Human and Social Capital	Human Exploitation	Political/ Economic Structures
STRATEGIES	Hold individual accountable and use sanctions if necessary. Target individuals. Work first. Self-sufficiency Enhance language experience. Psychology of mind Treatment interventions Resiliency Work ethic Mentors Literacy Asset development Abstinence education Marriage promotion Caseload reductions	Hold individual and social service systems accountable. Use sanctions if necessary. Full employment, growth in labor market Education Skill development Anti-poverty programs for childcare, child support, healthcare, housing EITC (earned income tax credit) Regional planning Community action programs Head Start Workforce Investment Act Continuous growth One-stop centers	Hold the colonialists (white, northern elite) accountable. Community-based development Political organizing to win control over economic and political institutions	Hold political/ economic power structure accountable. Use economic disparity trends as a measure. Interdisciplinary approach to macroeconomic planning and policies Whole-system planning Enhance living standards. Redistribution of wealth in other direction Access to capital and ownership

www.ahaprocess.com

Research Continuum Conclusions

- There is valid research in all 4 areas.

- A continuum of strategies covering all 4 areas is needed.

- Ruby Payne's framework offers a way to understand economic issues, to do a critical analysis of poverty and prosperity.

Community Sustainability Grid

	Individual Behavior	Human and Social Capital	Human Exploitation	Political/ Economic Structures
Individual Action				
Agency Action				
Community Action				
Policy				

www.ahaprocess.com

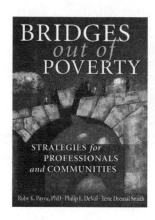

Key Points

OBJECTIVE

Establish key concepts that underlie *Bridges Out of Poverty* and aha! Process knowledge.

Key Points

- Poverty is relative.

- Poverty occurs in all races and in all countries.

- This workshop focuses on economic diversity, not racial or cultural diversity.

- Economic class is a continuous line, not a clear-cut distinction.

- Generational poverty and situational poverty are different.

- This work is based on patterns. All patterns have exceptions.

- An individual brings with him/her the hidden rules of the class in which he/she was raised.

- Schools and businesses operate from middle-class norms and use the hidden rules of middle class.

- For our clients to be successful, we must understand their hidden rules and teach them the rules that will make them successful at school, at work, and in the community.

- We can neither excuse persons from poverty nor scold them for not knowing; as professionals we must teach them and provide support, insistence, and expectations.

- In order to move from poverty to middle class or middle class to wealth, an individual must give up relationships for achievement (at least for some period of time).

- We cannot blame the victims of poverty for being in poverty.

- We cannot continue to support stereotypes and prejudices about the poor.

www.ahaprocess.com

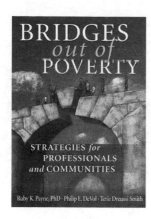

Hidden Rules

OBJECTIVE

Understand and give examples of the hidden rules of the 3 economic classes.

DRIVING FORCES

POVERTY

**Survival,
relationships,
entertainment**

MIDDLE CLASS

**Work, achievement,
material security**

WEALTH

**Financial, political, social
connections**

www.ahaprocess.com

POVERTY

Present most important

Decisions made for the moment based on feelings or survival

MIDDLE CLASS

Future most important

Decisions made against future ramifications

WEALTH

Traditions and history most important

Decisions made partially on basis of tradition/decorum

Tools

Future orientation, choice, and power

"If you choose, then you have chosen."

- What did you do?

- When you did that, what did you want?

- What are 4 other things you could have done instead?

- What will you do next time?

POVERTY

**Power linked to personal respect
Ability to fight
Can't stop bad things from happening**

MIDDLE CLASS

**Power/respect separated
Responds to position
Power in information and
    institutions**

WEALTH

**Power in expertise, connections
Power in stability
Influences policy and direction**

Tools

Relationship = power and respect

Relationships are often motivating factors.

Source: J. Pfarr Consulting

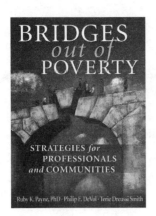

Language

OBJECTIVES

Distinguish the different registers of language and assist people in developing formal register.

Understand how language register, story structure, and language experience influence cognitive development.

Registers of Language

REGISTER	EXPLANATION
FROZEN	Language that is always the same. For example: Lord's Prayer, wedding vows, etc.
FORMAL	The standard sentence syntax and word choice of work and school. Has complete sentences and specific word choices.
CONSULTATIVE	Formal register when used in conversation. Discourse pattern not quite as direct as formal register.
CASUAL	Language between friends and is characterized by a 400- to 800-word vocabulary. Word choice general and not specific. Conversation dependent upon non-verbal assists. Sentence syntax often incomplete.
INTIMATE	Language between lovers or twins. Language of sexual harassment.

Adapted from Martin Joos' research by Ruby K. Payne, *A Framework for Understanding Poverty*

KAPLAN DISCOURSE

FORMAL

CASUAL

STORY STRUCTURES

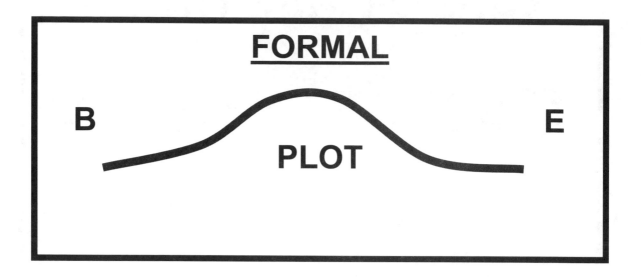

FORMAL

B

E

PLOT

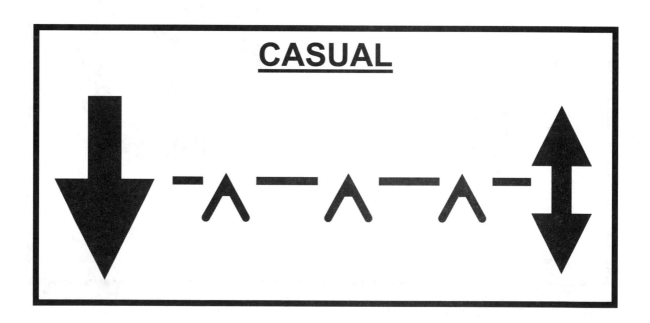

CASUAL

Research about language in children from ages 1 to 4 in stable households by economic group.

Number of words exposed to	Economic group	Affirmations (strokes)	Prohibitions (discounts)
13 million words	Welfare	1 for every	2
26 million words	Working class	2 for every	1
45 million words	Professional	6 for every	1

Source: *Meaningful Differences in the Everyday Experience of Young American Children* (1995) by Betty Hart & Todd R. Risley

If an individual depends upon a random episodic story structure for memory pattern, lives in an unpredictable environment, and does not have the ability to plan, then …

The individual **cannot plan.**

If an individual cannot plan, he/she **cannot predict.**

If an individual cannot predict, then he/she **cannot identify cause and effect.**

If an individual cannot identify cause and effect, he/she **cannot identify consequences.**

If an individual cannot identify consequences, he/she **cannot control impulsivity.**

If an individual cannot control impulsivity, he/she **has an inclination to criminal behavior.**

Teaching
Outside the Head

Learning
Inside the Head

Mediation

ASK

WHAT
Stimulus

WHY
Meaning

HOW
Strategy

Mental Prowess

VOICES

Child

Defensive, victimized, emotional, whining, losing attitude, strongly negative, non-verbal.

- Quit picking on me.
- You made me do it.
- I hate you.

Parent

Authoritative, directive, judgmental, evaluative, win-lose mentality, demanding, punitive, sometimes threatening.

- You shouldn't do that.
- Life's not fair. Get busy.

Adult

Non-judgmental, free of negative non-verbal, factual, often in question format, attitude of win-win.

- In what ways able to resolve?
- What are choices in this situation?

Adapted from work of Eric Berne, Games People Play

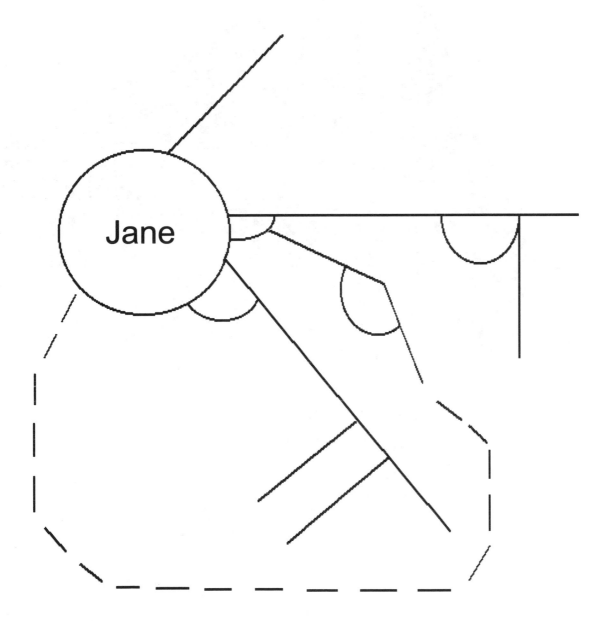

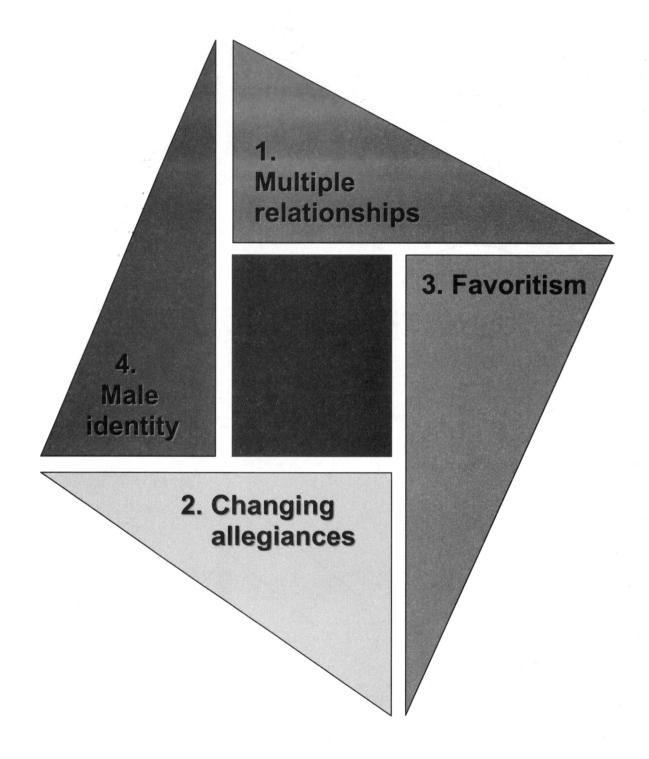

1.
Multiple
relationships

3. Favoritism

4.
Male
identity

2. Changing
allegiances

www.ahaprocess.com

believes that one is
fated or destined

↓

the behavior

↓

not get caught

↓

deny

↓

punished
forgiven

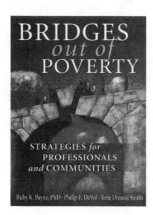

Resources

OBJECTIVES

- Analyze the 8 resources of the client/employee and make interventions based on those resources that are present.

- Understand that being stuck in poverty is often related to missing pieces; identify ways to build resources.

DEFINITION OF RESOURCES

FINANCIAL
Being able to purchase the goods and services of that class and sustain it.

EMOTIONAL
Being able to choose and control emotional responses, particularly to negative situations, without engaging in self-destructive behavior. Shows itself through choices.

MENTAL
Having the mental abilities and acquired skills (reading, writing, computing) to deal with daily life.

SPIRITUAL
Believing in (divine) purpose and guidance.

PHYSICAL
Having physical health and mobility.

SUPPORT SYSTEMS
Having friends, family, and backup resources available to access in times of need. These are external resources.

RELATIONSHIPS/ROLE MODELS
Having frequent access to adult(s) who are appropriate, **nurturing,** and who do not engage in destructive behavior.

KNOWLEDGE OF HIDDEN RULES
Knowing the unspoken cues and habits of a group.

www.ahaprocess.com

RESOURCES ADDED TO
Getting Ahead

Integrity and trust:
Your word is good, you do what you say you will do, and you are safe.

Motivation and persistence:
You have the energy and drive to prepare for, plan, and complete projects, jobs, and personal changes.

Formal register:
You have the emotional control, vocabulary, language ability, and negotiation skills to succeed in work and/or school settings.

DEFINITION OF POVERTY

To better understand
people from poverty,
the definition of poverty
will be
*"the extent to which an
individual does without
resources."*

Those resources are the
following …

DEFINITION OF RESOURCES

- **Connections, social networks, norms of reciprocity and trustworthiness**

- **Private and public aspects**
    - Bonding
    - Bridging
    - Thick and thin

Source: Bowling Alone: The Collapse and Revival of American Community *(2000) by Robert D. Putnam*

Social Capital

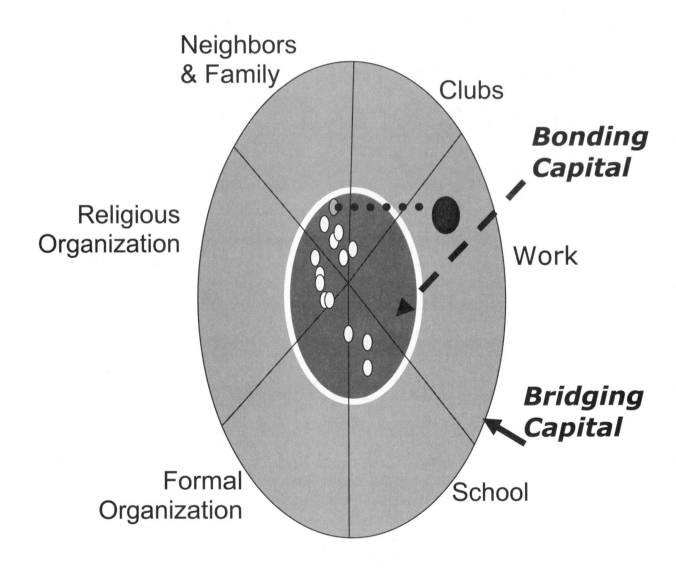

Neighbors & Family

Clubs

Bonding Capital

Religious Organization

Work

Bridging Capital

Formal Organization

School

QUESTIONS TO ASK ABOUT RESOURCES

FINANCIAL
Is $574 per month per person available? *
Is there enough income to cover all expenses?
Is your credit/debt ratio above 37%?
Do you spend more than 30% of your income on rent/mortgage?
Do you have enough savings to cover six months of expenses?
* Based on 125% of 2010 Poverty Guidelines for Family of Four: $27,563 per year/$2,297 per month.

EMOTIONAL
Is there evidence that the individual has persistence?
Does the individual have the words to express feelings in a way others can receive?
Does the individual have coping strategies (for adverse situations) that are not destructive to self or others?

MENTAL
Can the individual read, write, and compute?
Can the individual plan?
Can the individual problem-solve?
Can the individual understand cause and effect, then identify consequence?

SPIRITUAL
Does the individual believe in divine guidance and assistance?
Does the individual have belief in something larger than self?
Does the individual perceive an abstract and larger perspective that provides depth and meaning to life (culture, science, higher power, etc.)?

PHYSICAL
Can the individual take care of him-/herself without help?
Does the physical body allow the person to work and to learn?
Does the individual have transportation resources to get from one place to another?
Does the individual have health and wellness?

SUPPORT SYSTEMS AND SOCIAL CAPITAL
Who is the individual's bonding social capital? Is it positive?
Who is the individual's bridging social capital? Is it positive?

KNOWLEDGE OF MIDDLE CLASS HIDDEN RULES
Does this individual know the hidden rules of work and school?
How important are achievement and work?
Will this individual give up relationships for achievement (at least for some period of time)?

Defining Poverty

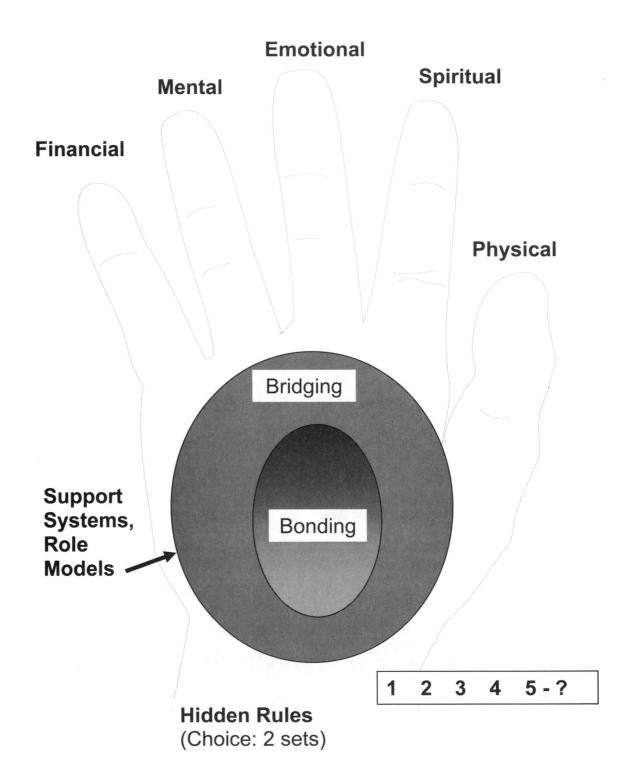

Emotional

Mental

Spiritual

Financial

Physical

Bridging

Support
Systems,
Role
Models

Bonding

1   2   3   4   5 - ?

Hidden Rules
(Choice: 2 sets)

www.ahaprocess.com

Mental Model of Resources

	Financial	Emotional	Mental	Spiritual	Physical	Support Systems	Relationships	Hidden Rules	Integrity	Motivation
5					▓					
4					▓					▓
3			▓		▓			▓	▓	▓
2	▓	▓	▓	▓	▓		▓	▓	▓	▓
1	▓	▓	▓	▓	▓	▓	▓	▓	▓	▓

Building Resources

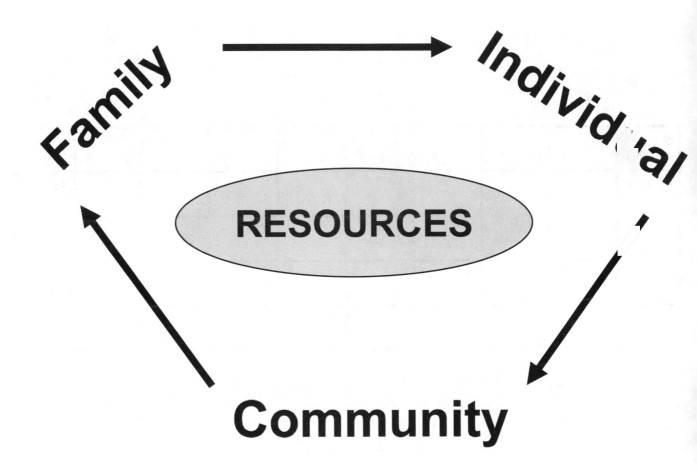

Source: J. Pfarr Consulting

www.ahaprocess.com

Theory of Change
for *Getting Ahead*

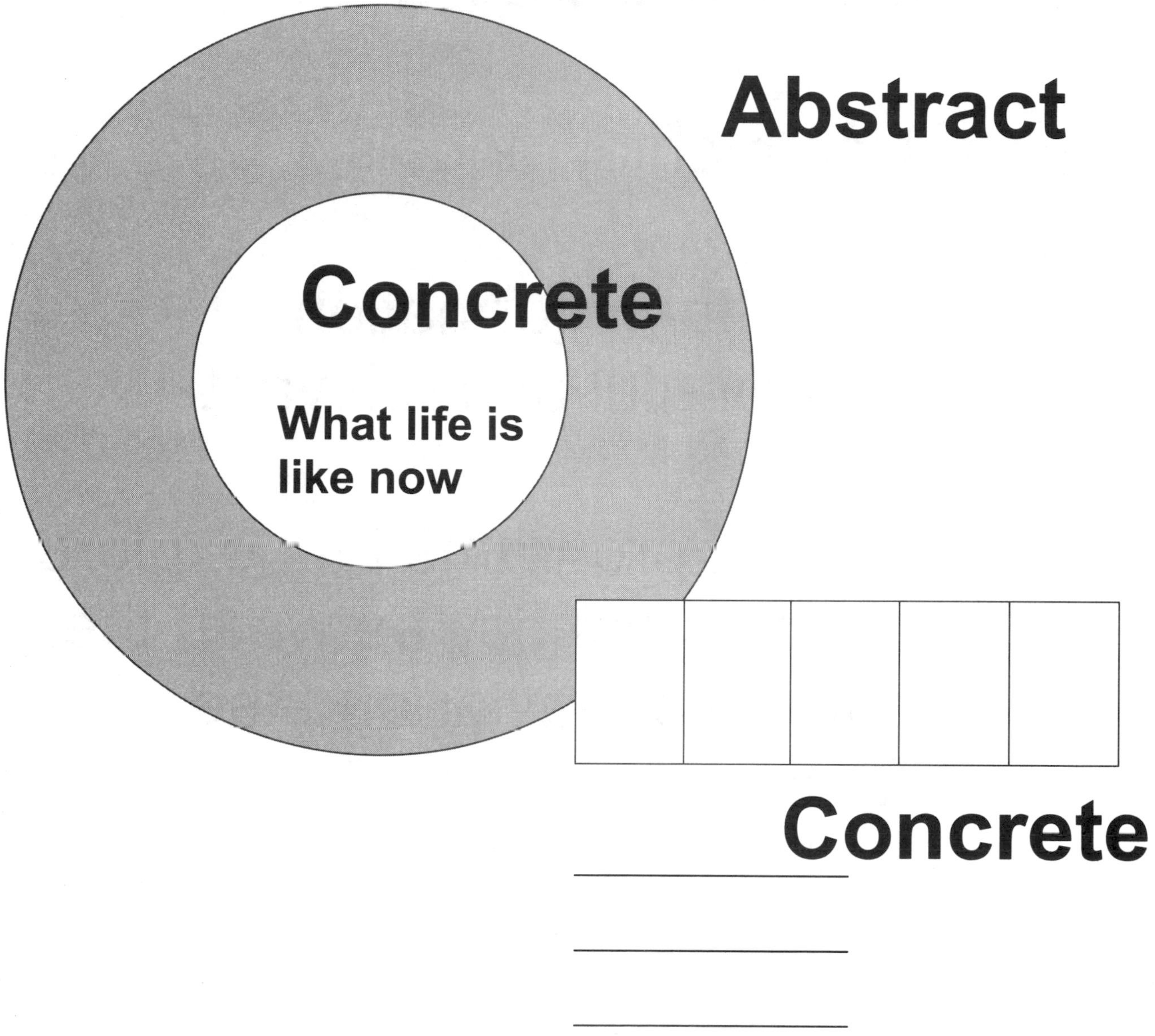

Abstract

Concrete

What life is like now

Concrete

_____

_____

_____

3 Ways to Move from the Concrete to the Abstract

- Use mental models.

- Make the information meaningful and relevant.

- Design programs that explore the discrepancy between the current behavior and the future story.

What the Abstract Consists of

Abstract

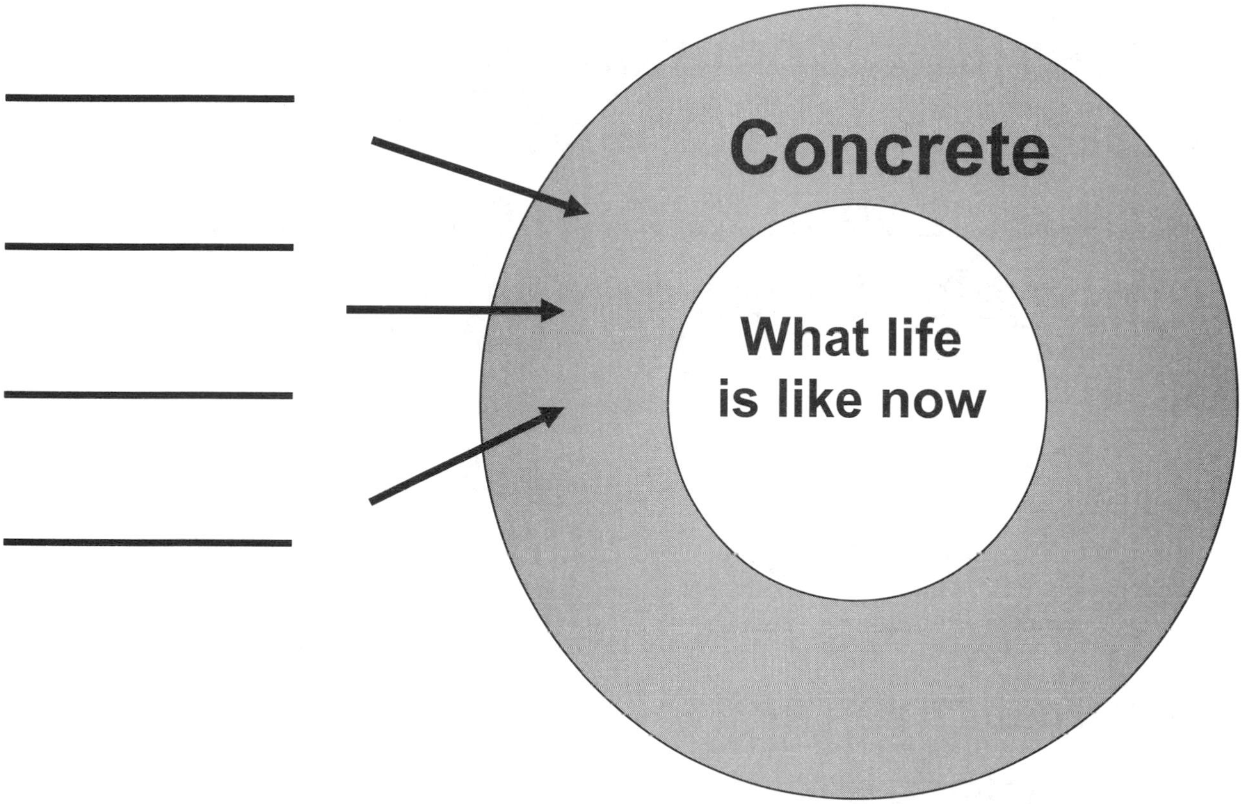

Concrete

What life
is like now

P	L	A	N	S

Concrete

Procedural Steps

_____

_____

_____

Learning Task:

Using the *Bridges* Approach

- Identify a common problem that people who come to your organization face (joblessness, homelessness, seeking food).

- Then fill in the *Bridges* Grid. Start with Individual Action and move across the row filling in ideas for what one might do to solve the problem.

- Then move down to the Agency Action, Community Action, and Policy rows and continue developing strategies.

Bridges Approach

Problem:_____

	Individual Behavior	Human and Social Capital	Exploitation	Political/ Economic Structures
Individual Action				
Agency Action				
Community Action				
Policy				

Processing

- What resources might the person want to build?

- What support can your agency provide?

- What supports might your community provide?

- What policy changes might be needed?

www.ahaprocess.com

Cascade Engineering

Welfare-to-career employee retention rates
- 1991–June 1999—29%
  December 1999—80%
- Annual retention rate through August 2010—71.5%

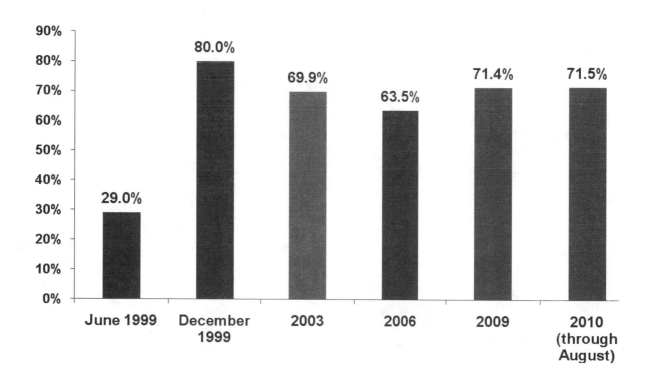

Cascade Engineering

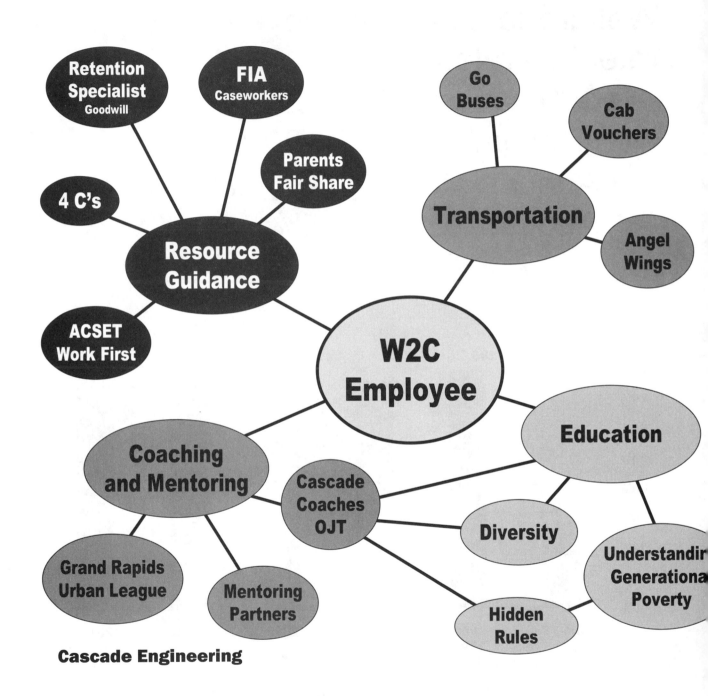

Retention Specialist
Goodwill

FIA
Caseworkers

Go
Buses

Cab
Vouchers

Parents
Fair Share

4 C's

Transportation

Resource
Guidance

Angel
Wings

ACSET
Work First

W2C
Employee

Education

Coaching
and Mentoring

Cascade
Coaches
OJT

Diversity

Grand Rapids
Urban League

Mentoring
Partners

Hidden
Rules

Understandin
Generationa
Poverty

Cascade Engineering

Mental Model for Community Prosperity

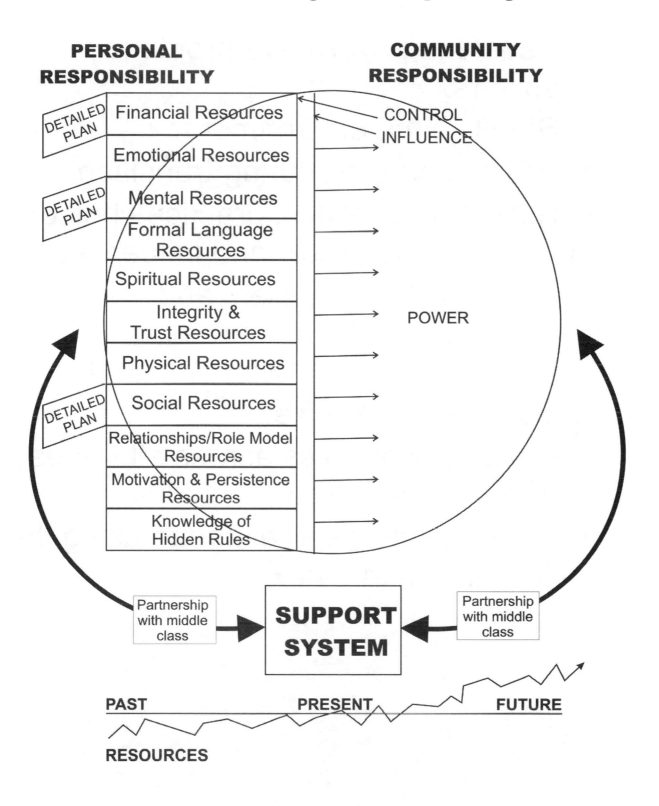

Principles of Change

- People in poverty are problem solvers.
- Stabilize the environment.
- Provide support during transition.
- Build future stories, practice choice, and develop power and influence.
- Communities, families, and individuals build resources.
- Bring members of all 3 economic classes to the table.
- Develop strategies across all 4 areas of research.
- Plan, monitor, and evaluate using the Social Health Index.

STRATEGIES

HIDDEN RULES	RESOURCES
I. Learn the rules of economic class in order to understand clients and employees who come from generational poverty. II. Teach the hidden rules; clients from poverty need to know two sets of hidden rules. III. Share the awareness of hidden rules with community partners. IV. Examine and re-examine your personal mental models about people in poverty to avoid stereotyping clients/employees. V. Use the understanding provided by awareness of hidden rules to counter stereotyping of people in poverty.	I. Examine the eight resources for individuals from poverty to become aware of internal strengths and environmental assets of clients and new hires. II. Build interventions on strengths. Look for the "half full" part of the glass. III. Engage individuals in poverty in solving community problems. IV. Provide economic opportunities for clients. Foster the development of small businesses. V. Create and support micro-credit opportunities. VI. Assist in the development of associations that are largely independent of agencies/institutions. VII. Refer clients to associations that match the individual's interests, skills, talents, and gifts.

FAMILY STRUCTURE	LANGUAGE, STORY STRUCTURE, AND COGNITION
I. Learn the rules of economic class in order to understand clients and employees who come from generational poverty. II. Provide additional support systems through associations, individual contact, and resource enhancement. III. Recognize that change takes time and happens in phases. IV. Provide long-term support and relationships. V. Recognize that some family members will resist change and may impede the efforts of individuals moving out of poverty. VI. Recognize that moving out of poverty may include a grieving process for some individuals. VII. Train front-line staff in the grief process so that they understand the emotional toll on clients and new hires. VIII. Recognize that domestic violence is more prevalent in poverty and that some clients may be at real risk during the change process.	I. Teach formal register to new hires and clients so that they become "bi-lingual." II. Encourage front-line staff to understand casual register. Staff must be able to translate forms and instructions from formal to casual register. III. Rewrite forms to be more meaningful. IV. Reduce middle-class "noise" by using meaningful mental models, drawings, stories, and analogies. V. Work with community partners to promote a rich language experience for children from birth to 3 years of age. VI. Reframe conflicts resulting from the use of casual register into learning experiences.

STRATEGIES

CREATING RELATIONSHIPS	SUPPORT SYSTEMS
I. Seek first to understand. II. Make deposits, not withdrawals. III. Appreciate humor and entertainment. IV. Respect relationships. V. Wait for the invitation. VI. Use the adult voice. VII. Use dialogue and discussion appropriately. VIII. Mediate. IX. Solve concrete problems. X. Be aware of one's own mental models. XI. Communicate without "noise." XII. Identify gifts, talents, and skills. XIII. Respect the importance of freedom of speech and personality. XIV. Think of people in poverty as the solution to problems.	I. Inventory individuals for gifts, talents, and skills. II. Inventory community associations, as well as service providers. III. Plan for long-term relationships. IV. Introduce individuals to others who have been successful and who have common interests. V. Recognize that change is a process, not an event. VI. Develop economic opportunities whenever possible.

MENTAL MODELS	MOTIVATION
I. Drawing, sketching. II. Time. III. Planning backward. IV. Formal register. V. Space. VI. Organizational change process. VII. Change process of each discipline. VIII. Limit situations. IX. Mental models for poverty and prosperity. X. Stories, metaphors, analogies. XI. Dealing with emotional blackmail. XII. Mediation.	I. Design structure. II. Reframe power struggles. III. Metaphor stories. IV. Voices. V. Health realization, psychology of the mind. VI. Managing emotional blackmail. VII. Reframe penance/forgiveness cycle. VIII. Behavioral analysis. IX. Win-win process.

www.ahaprocess.com

STRATEGIES

CO-EXISTING PROBLEMS	REDESIGN AND CQI (CONTINUOUS QUALITY IMPROVEMENT)
I. Identify barriers. II. Identify strengths. III. Asset development. IV. Capacity enhancement. V. Tucker Signing Strategies. VI. Best practices by discipline.	I. Theory of business. II. Client life cycle. III. Policy and procedure redesign. IV. Staff assignments. V. Orientation. VI. Engaging and inviting parents. VII. Utilizing information. VIII. Support growth of associations. IX. New-science strategies.

COMMUNITY STRATEGIES

I. Inventory of individuals.
II. Inventory of associations.
III. Inventory of service providers.
IV. Inventory of governmental agencies.
V. Identity connectors, mavens, salespeople.
VI. Community client life cycle.
VII. Make messages "sticky."
VIII. Change the context.
IX. Build partnerships with associations.
X. Build partnerships with providers.
XI. Cost benefits of collaboration.
XII. Provide resources as needed.
XIII. Provide economic opportunity.
XIV. Provide micro-credit.

Follow-Up Ideas

- Person-to-person changes:

- Organization changes:

- Community changes:

Bibliography—Suggested Reading

Brouwer, Steve. (1998). *Sharing the Pie: A Citizen's Guide to Wealth and Power in America*. New York, NY: Henry Holt & Company.

Covey, Stephen R. (1989). *The Seven Habits of Highly Effective People: Powerful Lessons in Personal Change*. New York, NY: Simon & Schuster.

de Soto, Hernando. (2000). *The Mystery of Capital: Why Capitalism Triumphs in the West and Fails Everywhere Else*. New York, NY: Basic Books.

Farson, Richard. (1997). *Management of the Absurd: Paradoxes in Leadership*. New York, NY: Touchstone.

Freedman, Jill, & Combs, Gene. (1996) *Narrative Therapy: The Social Construction of Preferred Realities*. New York, NY: W.W. Norton & Company.

Galeano, Eduardo. (1998). *Upside Down: A Primer for the Looking-Glass World*. New York, NY: Metropolitan Books.

Gladwell, Malcolm. (2000). *The Tipping Point: How Little Things Can Make a Big Difference*. Boston, MA: Little, Brown & Company.

Goleman, Daniel. (1995). *Emotional Intelligence*. New York, NY: Bantam Books.

Harrison, Lawrence E., & Huntington, Samuel P. (Eds.). (2000). *Culture Matters: How Values Shape Human Progress*. New York, NY: Basic Books.

Hart, Betty, & Risley, Todd R. (1995). *Meaningful Differences in the Everyday Experience of Young American Children*. Baltimore, MD: Paul H. Brookes Publishing Co.

Hawkins, Paul, Lovins, Amory, & Lovins, L.H. (1999). *Natural Capitalism: Creating the Next Industrial Revolution*. Boston, MA: Little, Brown & Company.

Hooks, Bell. (2000). *Where We Stand: Class Matters*. New York, NY: Routledge.

Kelly, Marjorie. (2001). *The Divine Right of Capital: Dethroning the Corporate Aristocracy*. San Francisco, CA: Berrett-Koehler Publishers, Inc.

Lareau, Annette. (2003). *Unequal Childhoods: Class, Race, and Family Life.* Berkeley, CA: University of California Press.

Levine, Mel. (2002). *A Mind at a Time.* New York, NY: Simon & Schuster.

Lind, Michael. (2004). Are we still a middle-class nation? *The Atlantic*. Volume 293. Number 1. January-February. pp 120–128.

Mattaini, Mark A. (1993). *More Than a Thousand Words: Graphics for Clinical Practice.* Washington, DC: NASW Press.

Miller, William R., & Rollnick, Stephen. (2002). *Motivational Interviewing: Preparing People for Change*. (Second Edition). New York, NY: Guilford Press.

O'Connor, Alice. (2001). *Poverty Knowledge: Social Science, Social Policy, and the Poor in Twentieth-Century U.S. History*. Princeton, NJ: Princeton University Press.

Oshry, Barry. (1996): *Seeing Systems: Unlocking the Mysteries of Organizational Life*. San Francisco, CA: Berrett-Koehler Publishers.

Putnam, Robert D. (2000). *Bowling Alone: The Collapse and Revival of American Community*. New York, NY: Simon & Schuster.

Sapolsky, Robert M. (1998). *Why Zebras Don't Get Ulcers: An Upated Guide to Stress, Stress-Related Diseases, and Coping*. New York, NY: W.H. Freeman & Company.

Senge, Peter M. (1994). *The Fifth Discipline: The Art and Practice of the Learning Organization*. New York, NY: Currency Doubleday.

Sharron, Howard, & Coulter, Martha. (1996). *Changing Children's Minds: Feuerstein's Revolution in the Teaching of Intelligence*. Birmingham, England: Imaginative Minds.

Shipler, David K. (2004). *The Working Poor: Invisible in America*. New York, NY: Alfred A. Knopf.

Stewart, Thomas A. (1997). *Intellectual Capital: The New Wealth of Organizations*. New York, NY: Currency Doubleday.

Stosny, Steven. (2003). *The Powerful Self*. Silver Spring, MD: Booksurge.

Taylor-Ide, Daniel, &Taylor Carl, E. (2002). *Just and Lasting Change: When Communities Own Their Futures*. Baltimore, MD: Johns Hopkins University Press.

Vella, Jane. (2002). *Learning to Listen Learning to Teach*: The Power of Dialogue in Educating Adults. San Francisco, CA: Jossey-Bass.

Warren, Elizabeth, & Warren Tyagi, Amelia. (2003). *The Two-Income Trap: Why Middle-Class Mothers and Fathers Are Going Broke*. New York, NY: Basic Books.

Additive Model:
The aha! Process Approach
to Building Sustainable Communities

by Philip DeVol

The mission of aha! Process, Inc. is to positively impact the education and lives of individuals in poverty around the world. This mission is informed by the reality of life in poverty, research on the causes of poverty, and Dr. Ruby K. Payne's research and insights into economic diversity. The issues that aha! Process addresses are economic stability; the development of resources for individuals, families, and communities; and community sustainability. aha! Process provides an additive model that recognizes people in poverty, middle class, and wealth as problem solvers. The focus is on solutions, shared responsibilities, new insights, and interdependence. This work is about connectedness and relationships; it is about "us."

Using the Knowledge of People in Poverty to Build
an Accurate Mental Model of Poverty

Going directly to people in generational poverty, the people working the low-wage jobs, and listening to them talk about their concrete experiences is to learn from the experts, the people with the knowledge. The circle of life for a family at the bottom of the economic ladder is intense and stressful. Cars and public transportation are unreliable and insufficient, low-wage jobs come and go, housing is crowded and very costly, time and energy go into caring for the sick and trying to get health care, and many of the interactions with the dominant culture are demeaning and frustrating. For people in poverty, the arithmetic of life doesn't work. Housing costs are so high and wages so low that people have to double up, usually with family members, but often with people they may not know very well. All the elements in this mental model of poverty are interlocking: When the car won't start it sets off a chain reaction of missed appointments, being late to work, losing jobs, and searching for the next place to live. Vulnerability for people in poverty is concrete. When the price of gas goes to $3.00 or more a gallon, it can mean having to work half a day to fill the tank. When one's attention is focused on the unfolding crisis of the day, people in poverty fall into what Paulo Freire calls the tyranny of the moment. Adds Peter Swartz: "The need to act overwhelms any willingness people have to learn." In this way poverty robs people of their future stories and the commitment to education. It requires them to use reactive skills, not true choice making, to survive. And finally, it robs them of power; the power to solve problems in such a way as to change the environment—or to make future stories come true.

By continuing to listen, one learns that people survive these circumstances by developing relationships of mutual reliance and facing down problems with courage and humor. It is family, friends, and acquaintances who give you a place to stay, food to eat, a ride to work, and help with your children. It's not Triple A that you call when your car breaks down; it's

Uncle Ray. People in poverty are the masters at making relationships quickly. Above all, they are problem solvers; they solve immediate, concrete problems all day long.

Unfortunately, the current operating mental model of our society appears to be that people in poverty are needy, deficient, diseased, and not to be trusted. Again, this can be learned by simply listening: listening to policymakers, commentators, and taxpayers who don't want their tax dollars to go to someone who isn't trying, isn't motivated, is lazy, and so on. Another way to discover the underlying mental model is to observe its programs in action and work backward. Three- to five-year lifetime limits for assistance, 90 days of services, work first … These policies point to frustration felt by those whose mental model of the poor is that they are needy, deficient, and diseased.

This inaccurate mental model is fed by media reports that favor soap operas to conceptual stories and individual stories to trends and the broader influences. The public hears about a fictitious "welfare queen" but not comprehensive studies. What is needed is a thorough understanding of the research on poverty.

Studying Poverty Research to Further Inform the Work of aha! Process

David Shipler, author of *The Working Poor*, says that in the United States we are confused about the causes of poverty and, as a result, are confused about what to do about poverty (Shipler, 2004). In the interest of a quick analysis of the research on poverty, we have organized the studies into the following four clusters:

- *Behaviors of the individual*
- *Human and social capital in the community*
- *Exploitation (including colonial exploitation)*
- *Political/economic structures*

For the last four decades discourse on poverty has been dominated by proponents of two areas of research: those who hold that the *true* cause of poverty is the behaviors of individuals and those who hold that the *true* cause of poverty is political/economic structures. The first argues that if people in poverty would simply be punctual, sober, and motivated, poverty would be reduced if not eliminated. For them, the answer is individual initiative. Voter opinion tends to mirror the research. Forty percent of voters say that poverty is largely due to the lack of effort on the part of the individual (Bostrom, 2005). At the other end of the continuum, the argument is that globalization, as it is currently practiced, results in the loss of manufacturing jobs, forcing communities to attract business by offering the labor of their people at the lowest wages, thus creating a situation where a person can work full time and still be in poverty. In a virtual dead heat with the countering theory, 39 percent of voters think that poverty is largely due to circumstances beyond the individual's control. Unfortunately, both two sides tend to make either/or assertions as if to say, *It's either this or that—as if "this" is true and "that" is not.*

Either/or assertions have not served us well; it must be recognized that causes of poverty are a both/and reality. Poverty is caused by both the behaviors of the individual and political/economic structures—and everything in between. Definitions for the four clusters of research and sample topics are provided in the table below.

CAUSES OF POVERTY			
Behaviors of the Individual	**Human and Social Capital in the Community**	**Exploitation**	**Political/Economic Structures**
Definition: Research on the choices, behaviors, characteristics, and habits of people in poverty.	*Definition:* Research on the resources available to individuals, communities, and businesses.	*Definition:* Research on how people in poverty are exploited because they are in poverty.	*Definition:* Research on the economic, political, and social policies at the international, national, state, and local levels.
Sample topics: Dependence on welfare Morality Crime Single parenthood Breakup of families Intergenerational character traits Work ethic Racism and discrimination Commitment to achievement Spending habits Addiction, mental illness, domestic violence Planning skills Orientation to the future Language experience	*Sample topics:* Intellectual capital Social capital Availability of jobs Availability of well-paying jobs Racism and discrimination Availability and quality of education Adequate skill sets Childcare for working families Decline in neighborhoods Decline in social morality Urbanization Suburbanization of manufacturing Middle-class flight City and regional planning	*Sample topics:* Drug trade Racism and discrimination Payday lenders Sub-prime lenders Lease/purchase outlets Gambling Temp work Sweatshops Sex trade Internet scams	*Sample topics:* Globalization Equity and growth Corporate influence on legislators Declining middle class De-industrialization Job loss Decline of unions Taxation patterns Salary ratio of CEO to line worker Immigration patterns Economic disparity Racism and discrimination

Typically, communities put a great deal of effort into the first area of research: the behaviors of the individuals. "Work first" was one of the key themes of the welfare reform act of 1996. TANF (Temporary Assistance to Needy Families) organizations focused on getting people to work. The idea was that getting a job, any job, and learning to work were more important than going to job-training classes or receiving treatment. Community agencies offered treatment for substance abuse and mental-health problems, money-management classes, and programs to address literacy, teen pregnancies, language experience, and more. The mission of these agencies is not to work directly on poverty issues but to deal with co-existing problems. All of these agencies encourage their clients to change behaviors, recording and managing the changes through the use of plans and contracts, and often sanction clients who fail to adhere to treatment plans.

Community efforts to enhance human and social capital include the strategies found in Head Start, WIA programs, One-Stop centers, Earned Income Tax Credit, and other anti-poverty programs. In this area too, accountability and sanctions are used to measure and motivate community organizations. Schools that don't meet certain benchmarks are taken over by state departments; TANF organizations that don't meet certain benchmarks don't receive incentive funds. This isn't to make a blanket criticism of any of the programs that serve low-wage workers. In fact, many programs have great value to those who have used them. Rather, it's the almost exclusive focus on these two areas of research that is the problem.

Communities rarely develop strategies to restrict, replace, or sanction those who exploit people in poverty. Even those organizations charged with fighting poverty sometimes neglect this cause of poverty. In part, this comes from departmentalizing community services. People who work in organizations charged with serving those in poverty don't think of exploiters as their responsibility. That falls to law enforcement and policymakers.

Departmentalizing is even more pronounced when it comes to the causes of poverty that arise from political and economic structures. Community economic development is left to the market system, developers, businesses, corporations, the Chamber of Commerce, and elected officials. People who typically work with those in poverty don't see a role for themselves in the debate on economic development issues any more than those who are engaged in business ventures make a direct connection between their work and the well-being of people in poverty. And yet, in concrete terms, there is a direct connection between quality of life and the actions of government and business. For the person in poverty it comes down to this: A person can get vocational training in a particular skill, get a job, and still be in poverty.

This all-too-common reality is the reason why communities must develop strategies across all four areas of research, not just the first two. To continue to focus exclusively on the first two areas of research is to invite more of the same—in short, more poverty. There is good research in all four areas; communities must develop strategies in all four areas if they are going to build resources and sustainability.

Alice O'Connor, author of *Poverty Knowledge*, says our society has typically looked at poverty through the prism of race and gender. She suggests that another analytic category is needed, that of economic class (O'Connor, 2001). In her seminal 1996 work *A Framework for Understanding Poverty*, Ruby Payne offered that prism. Since then aha! Process has published many books and produced many videos and workbooks that are used to address poverty across all four areas of research.

www.ahaprocess.com

The Need for Change: Naming Problems and Finding Solutions

Any community or organization that sets out to address poverty, education, health care, justice, or community sustainability must acknowledge that it seeks change: change in the individual's behavior, change in community approaches, and/or change in political/economic structures. Put another way, there is no agency that receives money—be it federal, state, or private—to keep behaviors and conditions exactly as they are. We seek change because we perceive something to be wrong.

Naming the problem is the first step toward a solution, and the most important step, for if the problem is not named accurately the course of action based on that faulty assumption will only lead further and further from a solution. So naming problems accurately—making the correct diagnosis—is crucial because it is on those definitions that the theories of change and program activities are based.

But naming the problem isn't as simple as it seems. If a problem exists, is it due to something that is lacking, a shortage, a disadvantage, a handicap? It is here that planners, providers, and problem solvers tend to slide into what often is referred to as the deficit model. This model seems to derive from what William Miller calls the righting reflex. He says, "Human beings seem to have a built-in desire to set things right" (Miller, 2002). We see something that is wrong; we want to fix it. This tendency is all well and good as long as it's confined to one's own problems, but as soon as our fix-it intentions are focused on others, this approach quickly loses its charm and questions arise. Who is it that names the problem? Who is it a problem for? What evidence is provided? How broad or deep is the investigation? People from minority cultures and dominated groups are the first to ask these questions, for it is often their ways of raising children, their language uses, and their problem-solving strategies that are being labeled as having deficits by the mainstream culture. Nobody likes deficit labeling. So it is that the righting reflex leads to deficit models that few of us like—and even fewer defend, for good reasons.

There is no known father or mother of the deficit model. Nobody claims it, but the title or slur gets hung around the neck of those who use it, or appear to use it. Some people hold that James Coleman, who has been called the "father of busing," proposed a deficit model. A review of the body of his work would refute that label. His research on education, one of the largest research projects ever undertaken, discussed economic class and achievement in its complexities. It was legislators, businesspeople, school administrators, and others who were under pressure to "Fix it!" who simplified Coleman's work when they turned it into policy. There are two things to be learned from this. First, the deficit model is simplistic; it oversimplifies the research and applies the righting reflex. Second, there is research—and then there are those who use the research.

It's important to take a closer look at how problems get named and what the distinction is between naming problems and deficit labeling. The deficit model names the problem and blames the individual; the individual must change, whereas society can be left unaltered. It is, however, possible to name problems and not blame the individual. For example, Dr. James P. Comer, not by any stretch a proponent of the deficit model, does identify the family environment as crucial to a child's academic success. He points to hard science—brain research—that confirms the interactive process between the mediation (interpretation of reality) that children receive from caregivers before they come to school with the continuous mediation when children enter school. Quoting Comer: "Without [mediation] children can lose the 'sense'—the intelligence potential—they were born with. Children who have had positive developmental experiences before starting school acquire a set of beliefs, attitudes, and values—as well as social, verbal, and problem-solving skills, connections, and power— that they can use to succeed in school. They are the ones best able to elicit a positive response from people at school and bond with them." Read another way, this could appear as labeling low-income families with deficits. Of course, it isn't that because Comer acknowledges the problems that exist across the system; it's never as simple as the fault of a single person or group. The body of Comer's work reveals the true nature of his model (Comer, 2001).

Despite the fact that the deficit model seems to have no father or mother and is the work of policymakers more than researchers (and gets confused with the naming of problems), the deficit model is still for real. Its features are that it fixes the problems on the individual and therefore focuses on fixing the individual. Environmental conditions are translated into the characteristics of the individual and gradually turn into negative stereotypes. The talents, gifts, and skills of an individual get lost. In the deficit model the "glass is seen as half empty." The message becomes "you can't," and the impulse to care for and protect arises. Thus we have "special needs," "special programs," "special rooms," and "special personnel," all of which can lead to and foster dependency.

The lack of staff training can result in the deficit model appearing in the attitudes of the professionals, in individual bias, and inaccurate assumptions. Notes Comer: "Many successful people are inclined to attribute their situations to their own ability and effort— making them, in their minds, more deserving than less successful people. They ignore the support they received from families, networks of friends and kin, schools, and powerful others. They see no need for improved support of youth development" (Comer, 2001). Without training, staff members are likely to see deficits where there are none. A child who comes to school after getting up early to pump water from an outside well and whose mother hand-washes clothes once a week may be seen as dirty, less presentable, more lacking in physical resources than children who can shower in their own bathroom before coming to school and whose mother uses a washer and dryer. The first child has the resources and skills but isn't readily able to demonstrate those capabilities.

The lack of understanding on the part of the staff can lead to labeling that is hard to shake. If the school or agency doesn't provide some way for individuals to demonstrate their skills and resources, the glass will always appear to be half empty.

Problems are identified with student performance, drug use, teen pregnancy, inadequate skill sets, job retention, criminal behavior, poverty, and so on, all of which gives rise to fix-it programs. One Teacher Leaders Network online discussion participant offered this analogy about deficit-model programs: "We call it the 'chicken inspector' mindset. You see, the chicken inspector has been trained to look for something that isn't right, so that's his focus and that's what he finds—the things that are wrong. The more things he finds wrong, the better he feels he is doing his job."

The deficit model finds its way into the design of programs. Legislators and professionals set policy and create departments and programs. Each department is expected to fix the piece of the pie that falls under its purview. These reactions to the latest problem set up a random approach to problem solving and result in remedial programs focused on the behaviors of the individual while losing sight of the whole system made up of families, neighborhoods, communities, and sociopolitical/economic structures.

This isn't to suggest that policymakers and program designers set out to apply the deficit model. It's more likely that they select some other approach but for any number of reasons fail to adhere to their espoused theory (what is said) and slide into a "theory of use" (what is done) that resembles the deficit model (Senge, 1994). Perhaps the most common reason for this slip is that it's easier to describe, plan for, monitor, and sanction the behaviors of individuals than it is to hold organizations, communities, and systems accountable in the same way (Washburne, 1958). The fact is that the deficit model is resilient, and we slide back into it easily.

Opposite the deficit model are many models that offer what the deficit model does not. They go by many names: positive model, developmental assets, competency, value-based, and strength-based … to name a few. Other models have been assigned names by their developers: Health Realization, Resiliency in Action, Comer Model, and Motivational Interviewing to name but four. Each of these models has its distinct theory and practices, but the one thing they have in common is that they see "the glass as half full."

Positive models too are not without their critics. For example, child-protection workers point out that reframing the behaviors and characteristics of victims of abuse into strengths is naïve. No matter how resilient the child, the fact remains that the child has very little control over his/her environment and the behaviors of adults. Educators note that children in poverty have been exposed to more in their few years than many adults. In some ways they seem to have adult capabilities; they take care of themselves and feel confident they can handle big decisions. But the educators caution against accepting this claim. According to a recent piece by Craig Sautter, "We as adults need to remember that they are not adults. They still have a lot of growing and developing to do and still need the guidance of adults who can be there to help them through their growing-up period" (Sautter, 2005).

Deficit Models   **Positive Models**

The additive model, a term used by Ruby Payne to describe the work of her company, aha! Process, combines the value of accurate problem identification with a positive, strength-based, communitywide approach to change. Applying the glass half empty/half full model to the three economic classes and the work of aha! Process would look like this:

For the Person in Poverty

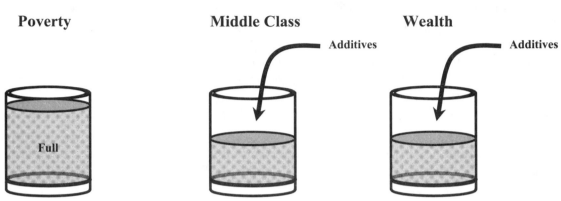

To survive in poverty, individuals must have reactive, sensory, and non-verbal skills. This means they have the ability to read situations, establish relationships, and solve immediate and concrete problems quickly. In that environment, individuals have a full glass; they have the assets and strengths to survive.

When individuals in poverty encounter the middle-class world of work, school, and other institutions, they do not have all the assets necessary to survive in that environment because what is needed there are proactive, abstract, and verbal skills. The additive model offers insight into how hidden rules of economic class work, along with a framework for building resources, a way to fill up the glass.

When the person in middle class encounters wealth, the same is true—but to a greater extent.

For the Person in Middle Class

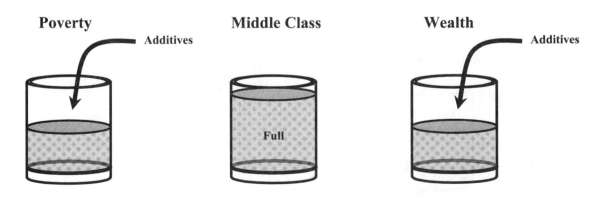

www.ahaprocess.com

Individuals raised in a middle-class environment learn the hidden rules, mindsets, and means of survival the same way persons in poverty or wealth do: through osmosis. To learn the survival rules of one's environment, virtually all one has to do is breathe. So the glass is full so long as individuals remain in their environment. But should those persons suddenly find themselves in poverty—or even in a poverty neighborhood—would they have the assets needed to survive there? The glass would be half empty. But there is a more common scenario that brings people in middle class and people in poverty together; that is in the institutions run by middle-class people. In this scenario both groups come with a glass half full because they may not understand the rules or value the assets of the other person or the other class. Here is where the additive model can help. It names the problem and offers insight and awareness; it opens the way to build relationships and eventually to better outcomes for both.

As middle-class individuals interact with people in wealth they may not know any more about the rules of survival in wealth than the person in poverty knows about the rules of middle class (and how the values of the additive model apply).

For the Person in Wealth

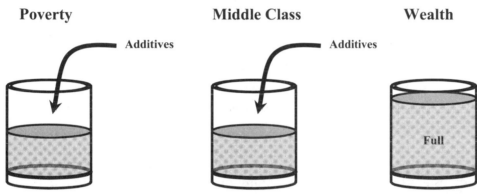

| Poverty | Middle Class | Wealth |

The additive model has something to offer people in wealth as well. Where the worlds of wealth, middle class, and poverty intersect, the additive model can assist. Due to their connections, influence, and power, people in wealth often are in the position to design the policies and directions of the institutions that the middle class run and that the people in poverty use. If wealthy individuals' poverty and middle-class glass is only half full and all they know is their own rules of survival, then it can result in policies that are ineffective and counterproductive.

To better understand the additive model, we must consider aha! Process definitions and core concepts.

Resources

Resources: The following resources are quality-of-life indicators that are described in almost all aha! Process publications.

Financial	Physical
Emotional	Support systems
Mental	Relationships/role models
Spiritual	Knowledge of hidden rules

Poverty: the extent to which an individual or community does without these resources.

Prosperity/sustainability: the extent to which an individual or community has these resources.

By these definitions it is easy to see that an individual may have low financial resources and at the same time have other resources that are very high. Of course, the opposite is true too: One can have high financial resources and be impoverished in other ways.

This approach emphasizes that every individual's story is different and takes into account the culture in which one lives. And yet, as a general rule, the additive model holds that to have high resources is better than to not have high resources. It's preferable to have financial stability than to be unable to pay for basic needs. It's preferable to have many positive relationships than to live in isolation. It's preferable to be able to identify feelings, choose behaviors, and get along with others than to be emotionally destructive.

The additive model holds that:
- Resources are to be developed by communities, families, and individuals. In fact, it is the appropriate role, or "job" if you will, of individuals, families, and communities to grow resources for oneself, one's family, and the community.
- The optimal way to build resources is to build on one's strengths. Focusing on low resources, weaknesses, and what is absent not only is no fun, it simply isn't effective.
- We must develop resource-building strategies across all four areas of poverty research. The deficit model is at work when a community focuses its anti-poverty strategies on the behaviors of the individual.

Ruby Payne's research on the hidden rules of economic class is another key component of the aha! Process approach. It is this analytic category that provides a new lens through which to examine poverty and prosperity issues. Again, some definitions will help clarify the additive model.

Hidden Rules of Economic Class

Hidden rules: the unspoken cues and habits of a group. All groups have hidden rules; you know you belong when you don't have to explain anything you say or do. These rules are held by racial, ethnic, religious, regional, and cultural groups … to name a few. An individual's cultural fabric is made up of many threads, one of which is economic class. Where the threads are woven together the different cultures act on behaviors of the individual and group. Of these rules, economic class is a surprisingly strong thread, one that is often overlooked—or at least minimized.

The additive model holds that:

- The hidden rules arise from the environment in which a person lives, that they help persons survive in the class in which they were raised. This means that the rules of class are not to be criticized, but that we simply add options, new rules, a wider range of responses, an ability to negotiate more environments. While these are framed as choices and not identity, any individuals who begin to work on achievements—such as economic stability, education, or getting sober—are changing their identity. How they make the transition is a choice: Will they stay connected with people from their past, or will they move into new circles? This is an individual and often painful choice/process. Being aware of the choice can smooth the process, whatever the decision.
- It is beneficial for middle class people to learn the hidden rules of poverty—and not just so they're able to help people in poverty make changes, but because the hidden rules of poverty have value in their own right. Perhaps first among these is the value of relationships and the time given to them. The ability people in poverty have to establish quick but intimate relationships is an asset. In the additive model, change takes place, not just in the individual but in the theories of change and program designs of organizations. Middle-class organizations often have based their work on middle-class mindsets without an adequate mental model of poverty or knowledge of the hidden rules of the people they serve.

It is by adding to the hidden rules that one is raised with that people develop a range of responses that will give them control over their situations and open doors to new opportunities.

Language Issues

The aha! Process approach calls for an extensive discussion of language issues, including definitions of the registers of language, discourse patterns, story structures, language experience in the first three years of life, cognitive issues, and strategies to deal with all of these. As a body of work, aha! Process's many books, workbooks, videos, classroom strategies, and program-design strategies together make up a remarkable representation of the additive model. It is here that the model calls for an accurate naming of problems where the word deficit is used.

The additive model holds that:

- People build relationships by using the registers of language and discourse patterns skillfully.
- The strengths and uses of each register are encouraged where they can be most skillfully applied.
- Classroom interventions and agency strategies must be based on a clear understanding of the issues and a clear definition of the problems.
- The interventions themselves are built on the assets of the individual and the necessary changes fall as much on the professionals as on the individuals in poverty.
- Learning structures in the brain can be enhanced, but only by knowing the exact nature of the thinking that is occurring. In school settings the intervention cannot be random or general. The strategies offered by aha! Process are grade- and subject-specific.
- A rich language experience benefits children and prepares them for the world of work and school.
- Teachers value the language experience that children bring with them to school and prepare students to be able to skillfully navigate a wide range of language situations.
- In social service settings with adults, the additive model calls for the staff to become bilingual (able to translate from formal register to casual register).
- Change messages—be they about cardiovascular disease, breast feeding, birth weight, or the prevention of drug use—often taught in the formal register are now taught through a self-discovery process and by using mental models. Communication is meaningful and not just what Robert Sapolsky calls middle-class noise (Sapolsky, 1998).

Family Structure

Matriarchal structure: All families have capabilities and strengths, and all families are faced with demands. In the course of life all families must face suffering and hard times, but some families seem to have more than their share of suffering to contend with. Under ordinary demands and stressors, families will become stronger as a result of their struggles. But there are some things that can overrun and overwhelm a family's capabilities; those include chronic addiction, mental illness, physical illness, and poverty (Henderson, 1996). People in poverty sometimes contend with more than poverty alone, and poverty itself is so stressful that there is a direct correlation between poverty and stress-related illnesses (Sapolsky, 1998). In high-demand conditions, families take on a structure that fits the survival needs of the family. In that context, the matriarchal structure and associated patterns of behavior are assets, but if viewed in light of a deficit model are often seen as negative or even as lacking in morals. A matriarchal family is not synonymous with a dysfunctional family. As in all economic classes, dysfunctional things may happen, but living in poverty does not equate with dysfunctional behaviors. The additive model provides an understanding and appreciation of matriarchal families and offers new information and ways of increasing resources.

The additive model holds that:
- Family structures evolve to meet the survival needs of the family and that they are strengths.
- As with aha! Process knowledge, awareness gives people optional ways to stabilize the chaotic circle of life, to envision new patterns and stories, to practice choice, and to build new resources.

Sharing aha! Process Knowledge with Adults in Poverty

Co-investigation: Sharing aha! Process knowledge with people in poverty is done through a group investigation of the causes of poverty, examining the impact of poverty on the individual, and exploring new information. Individuals in the group assess their own resources and make plans to build their own future story. Here's one way of articulating the challenges faced by people in poverty:

Poverty traps people in the tyranny of the moment, making it very difficult to attend to abstract information or plan for the future (Freire, 1999; Sharron, 1996; Galeano, 1998)— *the very things needed to build resources and financial assets. There are many causes of poverty, some having to do with the choices of the poor, but at least as many stemming from community conditions and political/economic structures* (O'Connor, 2001; Brouwer, 1998; Gans, 1995).

The additive model holds that:
- People in poverty need an accurate perception of how poverty impacts them and an understanding of economic realities as a starting point both for reasoning and for developing plans for transition (Freire, 1999; Galeano, 1998).
- Using mental models for learning and reasoning, people can move from the concrete to the abstract (Freedman, 1996; Harrison, 2000; Sharron, 1996; Mattaini 1993; Jaworski, 1996; Senge, 1994).
- People can be trusted to make good use of accurate information, presented in a meaningful way by facilitators who provide a relationship of mutual respect and act as co-investigators (Freire, 1999; Sapolsky, 1998; McKnight, 1995; Pransky, 1998; Farson, 1997).
- Using Ruby Payne's definition of the resources necessary for a full life, as well as her insights into the hidden rules of economic class, people can evaluate themselves and their situation, choose behaviors, and make plans to build resources (Miller, 2002).
- The community must provide services, support, and meaningful opportunities during transition and over the long term (Putnam, 2002; Kretzmann, 1993).
- In partnership with people from middle class and wealth, individuals in poverty can solve community and systemic problems that contribute to poverty (Phillips, 2002; Kretzmann, 1993).

aha! Process Knowledge and Community Sustainability

Community sustainability: This is an issue that all communities, states, and nations must now face. The world has seen several revolutionary changes: the change from hunter/gatherer societies to agriculture, the industrial revolution, the information age, and now the era in which we must determine how to use our resources and live in our environment—and yet retain vital resources for our children and grandchildren.

The mission of aha! Process—to directly impact the education and lives of individuals in poverty around the world—leads to a role in this revolution. Communities are awakening to the reality that they do not offer a sustainable way of life to their children and are looking for direction. Equity and critical mass impact the changes that are taking place. If a community allows any group to be disenfranchised for any reason (religion, race, class), the entire community becomes economically poorer (Sowell, 1998). When poverty reaches the point of critical mass in a community and efforts to reverse the problem don't succeed, the people with the most resources tend to move out of the community, leaving behind enclaves of poverty. At this point the community is no longer sustainable.

Responding to the impending crisis with the mindset that created it and with the strategies that have been used to address poverty to date is to invite more of the same results: more poverty and more communities at risk.

aha! Process defines community as any group that has something in common and the potential for acting together (Taylor-Ide 2002). The rich social capital that peaked in the post-World War II era—and that has been on the decline since—must be restored (Putnam, 2000). The barn-raising metaphor for communities where citizens contribute to the building of the barn with their particular skills, gifts, and talents must replace the vending-machine metaphor, which is currently in use. The vending-machine metaphor reduces community members to consumers or shoppers who put 75 cents into the machine expecting 75 cents of goods and services in return. With that mindset, it's no surprise that we find people kicking, shaking, and cursing the vending machine.

The additive model holds that:
- It's better to be a barn raiser than a consumer.
- All three classes must be at the table.
- Communities must have a shared understanding and a common vocabulary to build critical mass that is willing and motivated to make the necessary changes.
- Strategies must cover all the causes of poverty—from the behaviors of individuals to political/economic structures.
- Communities must build intellectual capital.
- Long-term plans of 20 to 25 years are needed.
- Quality-of-life indicators must be monitored and reported regularly in the same way hat economic indicators are monitored and reported.

Conclusion

aha! Process offers a unique understanding of economic diversity that can give individual, families, and communities new ways of solving problems. It is the hope of aha! Process that 100 years from now poverty will no longer be viewed as economically inevitable. Two hundred years ago slavery was thought to be an economic necessity. It was not. One hundred fifty years ago it was believed that women were not capable of voting. That also was not true. We fervently hope that by 2100 individuals and society at large will no longer believe that poverty is inevitable. It is only by applying an additive model that we will understand and address both poverty and the underlying factors that have perpetuated it.

Works Cited

Andreas, Steve, & Faulkner, Charles. (Eds.). (1994). *NLP: The New Technology of Achievement*. New York, NY: Quill.

Bostrom, Meg. (2005). Together for Success: Communicating Low-Wage Work as Economy, Not Poverty. Ford Foundation Project. Douglas Gould & Co.

Brouwer, Steve. (1998). *Sharing the Pie: A Citizen's Guide to Wealth and Power in America*. New York, NY: Henry Holt & Company.

Comer, James P. (2001). Schools that develop children. *The American Prospect*. Volume 12. Number 7. April 23.

DeVol, Philip E. (2004). *Getting Ahead in a Just-Gettin'-by World: Building Your Resources for a Better Life*. Highlands, TX: aha! Process.

Farson, Richard. (1997). *Management of the Absurd: Paradoxes in Leadership*. New York, NY: Touchstone.

Freedman, Jill, & Combs, Gene. (1996). *Narrative Therapy: The Social Construction of Preferred Realities*. New York, NY: W.W. Norton & Company.

Freire, Paulo. (1999). *Pedagogy of the Oppressed*. New York, NY: Continuum Publishing Company.

Fussell, Paul. (1983). *Class: A Guide Through the American Status System*. New York, NY: Touchstone.

Galeano, Eduardo. (1998). *Upside Down: A Primer for the Looking-Glass World*. New York, NY: Metropolitan Books.

Gans, Herbert J. (1995). *The War Against the Poor*. New York, NY: Basic Books.

Harrison, Lawrence E., & Huntington, Samuel P. (Eds.). (2000). *Culture Matters: How Values Shape Human Progress*. New York, NY: Basic Books.

Henderson, Nan. (1996). *Resiliency in Schools: Making It Happen for Students and Educators*. Thousand Oaks, CA: Corwin Press.

Jaworski, Joseph. (1996). *Synchronicity: The Inner Path of Leadership*. San Francisco, CA: Berrett-Koehler Publishers.

Kahlenberg, Richard, D. (2001). Learning from James Coleman. *Public Interest*. Summer.

Kretzmann, John, & McKnight, John. (1993). *Building Communities From the Inside Out: A Path Toward Finding and Mobilizing a Community's Assets.* Chicago, IL: ACTA Publications.

Lewis, Oscar. (1966). The Culture of Poverty. *Scientific American.* Volume 215. Number 4. pp. 19–25.

Mattaini, Mark A. (1993). *More Than a Thousand Words: Graphics for Clinical Practice.* Washington, DC: NASW Press.

McKnight, John. (1995). *The Careless Society: Community and Its Counterfeits.* New York, NY: Basic Books.

Miller, William R., & Rollnick, Stephen. (2002). *Motivational Interviewing: Preparing People for Change* (Second Edition). New York, NY: Guilford Press.

O'Connor, Alice. (2001). *Poverty Knowledge: Social Science, Social Policy, and the Poor in Twentieth-Century U.S. History.* Princeton, NJ: Princeton University Press.

Payne, Ruby K., DeVol, Philip, & Dreussi Smith, Terie. (2001). *Bridges Out of Poverty: Strategies for Professionals and Communities.* Highlands, TX: aha! Process.

Phillips, Kevin. (2002). *Wealth and Democracy: A Political History of the American Rich.* New York, NY: Broadway Books.

Pransky, Jack. (1998). *Modello: A Story of Hope for the Inner-City and Beyond.* Cabot, VT: NEHRI Publications.

Putnam, Robert D. (2000). *Bowling Alone: The Collapse and Revival of American Community.* New York, NY: Simon & Schuster.

Sapolsky, Robert M. (1998). *Why Zebras Don't Get Ulcers: An Updated Guide to Stress, Stress-Related Diseases, and Coping.* New York, NY: W.H. Freeman & Company.

Sautter, Craig. (2005). Who are today's city kids? Beyond the "deficit model." North Central Regional Educational Laboratory, a subsidiary of Learning Points Associates. http://www.ncrel.org/sdrs/cityschl/city1_1a.htm

Senge, Peter M. (1994). *The Fifth Discipline: The Art & Practice of the Learning Organization.* New York, NY: Currency Doubleday.

Sharron, Howard, & Coulter, Martha. (1996). *Changing Children's Minds: Feuerstein's Revolution in the Teaching of Intelligence.* Birmingham, England: Imaginative Minds.

Shipler, David K. (2004). *The Working Poor: Invisible in America.* New York, NY: Alfred A. Knopf.

Sowell, Thomas. (1998). Race, culture and equality. *Forbes.* October 5.

Sowell, Thomas. (1997). *Migrations and Cultures: A World View.* New York, NY: HarperCollins.

Taylor-Ide, Daniel, & Taylor, Carl, E. (2002). *Just and Lasting Change: When Communities Own Their Futures.* Baltimore, MD: Johns Hopkins University Press.

Washburne, Chandler. (1958). Conflicts between educational theory and structure. *Educational Theory.* Volume 8. Number 2. April.

About the Authors

Philip E. DeVol is a trainer, writer, consultant, and program designer specializing in community sustainability and poverty issues. In addition to co-authoring *Bridges Out of Poverty: Strategies for Professionals and Communities,* he authored *Getting Ahead in a Just-Gettin'-By World: Building Your Resources for a Better Life,* which is the foundation of a broader effort to engage individuals in solving community challenges through planning, teamwork, and a better understanding of resources. DeVol also works extensively with businesses, organizations, and communities to adapt innovative, high-impact *Bridges* strategies to their settings, as well as to build expertise, communication, and understanding among all parties. These efforts keep him in daily contact with people from all walks of life—and all political persuasions and beliefs—and build on nearly two decades of experience as director of an outpatient substance abuse treatment facility. Currently DeVol coordinates aha! Process, Inc. work with other organizations and agencies, working tirelessly to end poverty and build communities where everyone can do well. He lives in Ohio.

Terie Dreussi Smith is a gifted professional educator, trainer, and consultant, formerly serving as a public school teacher, as well as adjunct faculty member for several colleges where she focused on empowering adult students to make the transition out of poverty. She served as supervisor of prevention services at a community alcohol/drug treatment and prevention organization for more than nine years and was instrumental in the organization's redesign of programs and services for prevention and early intervention with clients from generational poverty. More recently Dreussi Smith has served as a consultant, grant writer, and social program manager for youth-based service agencies, community coalitions, and schools. As co-author of *Bridges Out of Poverty: Strategies for Professionals and Communities,* she has helped communities embed *Bridges* concepts by redesigning policies and services for families and young people in generational poverty. She lives in South Carolina.

Ruby K. Payne, Ph.D., author, speaker, publisher, business owner, and career educator, is an expert on the mindsets of economic classes and on crossing socioeconomic lines in education, work, and for social change. Her trailblazing efforts to address the needs of under-resourced people include dozens of publications, along with training programs that have served hundreds of thousands of educators at all levels. Her landmark book, *A Framework for Understanding Poverty,* has sold more than 1 million copies, and her collaboration with other educators has touched countless lives with practical, proven strategies for helping others succeed. Dr. Payne's work stems from more than two decades of firsthand experience in the public schools—as school department head, principal, and central office administrator of staff development, where she became known for helping students from all economic backgrounds to achieve academic success. As founder of aha! Process, Inc., Dr. Payne provides a wealth of research, training, and resources to the task of addressing the unique challenges faced by under-resourced people of all ages and backgrounds. She lives in Texas.

To find out more about these authors, *Bridges Out of Poverty* workshops,
and other resources, visit www.ahaprocess.com.

More eye-openers at ...
www.ahaprocess.com

- **Visit www.ahaprocess.com for our latest workshop offerings, including:**

  - Bridges into Health
  - *Investigations into Economic Class in America*
  - *Getting Ahead in a Just-Gettin'-By World*
  - Applying Bridges Concepts

- **Visit www.gettingaheadnetwork.com for more information on community-based models that will work where you live**

- **Look for Phil DeVol's latest book, co-authored with Karla Krodel: *Investigations into Economic Class in America* [Getting Ahead for college students]**

- **See another new release by DeVol: *Bridges to Sustainable Communities: A Systemwide, Cradle-to-Grave Approach to Ending Poverty in America* for techniques, training, and tips for generating Bridges Communities**

- **If you are interested in more information regarding seminars or training, we invite you to visit our website at www.ahaprocess.com**

- **Watch our website for the Bridges open-enrollment workshop schedule**

**For a complete listing of products, please visit
www.ahaprocess.com**